W9-BIQ-881

612
MCC

McCormick, Rosie.

Our bodies & art
activities.

$23   30002013

DATE DUE	BORROWER'S NAME	ROOM NUMBER
		20T
11/27/07	Jeanette	
11/X/08	Shequilla Cawley	308

BAKER & TAYLOR

Linking art to the world around us

Arty Facts

Our Bodies
& Art Activities

🌳 Crabtree Publishing Company
www.crabtreebooks.com

Crabtree Publishing Company

PMB 16A, 350 Fifth Avenue, Suite 3308
New York, NY
10118

612 Welland Avenue
St. Catharines, Ontario
L2M 5V6

Coordinating Editor: Ellen Rodger
Project Editors: P.A. Finlay, Carrie Gleason
Production Coordinator: Rosie Gowsell

Project Development and Concept Marshall Direct:
Editorial Project Director: Karen Foster
Editors: Claire Sippi, Hazel Songhurst, Samantha Sweeney
Researchers: Gerry Bailey, Alec Edgington
Design Director: Tracy Carrington
Designers: Flora Awolaja, Claire Penny, Paul Montague, James Thompson, Mark Dempsey,
Production: Victoria Grimsell, Christina Brown
Photo Research: Andrea Sadler
Illustrator: Jan Smith
Model Artist: Sophie Dean

Prepress, printing and binding by Worzalla Publishing Company

McCormick, Rosie.
  Our bodies and art activities / written by Rosie McCormick.
        p. cm. -- (Arty facts)
Includes index.
  Summary: Information about various topics related to the composition and
functioning of the human body forms the foundation for a variety of craft projects.
  ISBN 0-7787-1117-X (RLB) -- ISBN 0-7787-1145-5 (pbk.)
 1. Human anatomy--Juvenile literature. 2. Body, Human--Juvenile
literature. 3. Creative activities and seat work--Juvenile literature.
[1. Human anatomy. 2. Body, Human. 3. Handicraft.] I. Title. II.
Series.
  QM27 .M4234 2002
  612--dc21
                                    2002011632
                                    LC

Created by
Marshall Direct Learning

© 2002 Marshall Direct Learning

All rights reserved. No part of this publication may be reproduced, stored in a retrieval
system, or transmitted, in any form or by any means, electronic, mechanical, photocopying,
recording or otherwise, without prior written permission from the publisher.

FRONT COVER IMAGES: CNRI/ SCIENCE PHOTO LIBRARY; DAVID PARKER/ SCIENCE PHOTO LIBRARY; ALFRED PASIEKA/ SCIENCE PHOTO LIBRARY; KEREN SU/ CORBIS; TESSA HORTON/ SCIENCE PHOTO LIBRARY

Linking art to the world around us

Arty Facts
Our Bodies
& Art Activities

Contents

WRITTEN BY Rosie McCormick

Strong bones

A building needs a frame to hold it together, so does your body. The body's frame is called the skeleton. The skeleton is made up of more than 200 bones. Your skeleton gives your body its shape. Your skull gives your head its round shape. The bones in your limbs make them long and thin, and curved ribs shape your chest.

Protection

Some bones protect organs in the body. The skull protects the brain. The ribs protect the heart and lungs.

Moving frame

Your skeleton works with your muscles to allow you to move. Muscles are connected to your bones by stretchy bands called **tendons**. **Ligaments** pull bones to make them move.

Spongy bones

Bones have a hard protective covering on the outside. Inside is a layer of hard bone. In the center of the hard bone is a spongy layer that contains **marrow**. Thousands of **cells** are always busy rebuilding the bone to keep it strong. Cells also help the bone heal if it is broken.

Big and small

The longest and strongest bone in your skeleton is the femur, which is in your thigh. The smallest bone is the stirrup bone inside your ear.

Our Bodies

WHAT YOU NEED

styrofoam

black poster board

white poster board

glue

straws

scissors

white pencil

Skeleton man

Make a funny skeleton man with shiny bones to hang on your wall

1 With the white pencil, sketch the bones of a skeleton on black paper.

2 Cut matching skeleton bones from white poster board, straws, and styrofoam.

3

Glue the cut-out bones onto the black poster board to make a skeleton man.

Add extra details to your skeleton with a white pencil.

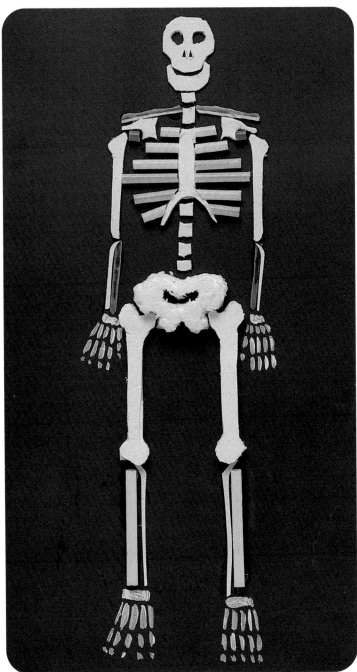

5

Art at our fingertips

If you press the tip of your finger onto an ink pad and then touch a piece of white paper, you will see your fingerprint. No one else in the world has fingerprints exactly like yours. Your footprints are also different from anyone else's.

Fingerprinting

A long time ago, slaves and prisoners were often marked by tattoos so they could be identified if they escaped. Many years later, photographs and body measurements were used to identify criminals. Fingerprinting was not developed until the 1880s, when scientists were able to show that it was almost impossible for two people to have the same fingerprint. Not long after, fingerprinting was introduced as a way of identifying criminals. Fingerprinting is an important tool in criminal investigations all over the world.

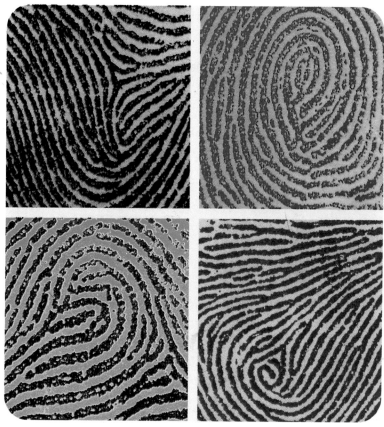

Everyone has a special fingerprint. Can you see the difference between these four patterns?

A magnified photograph of a fingertip showing the arch pattern.

Loops and arches

Look at your fingertips and you will see many tiny lines, or ridges. These loops and circles make patterns called fingerprints. Each finger has a different design. Scientists classify fingerprints into four groups by studying the pattern made by the ridges. In the "loop" group the ridges curve back over themselves. In the "whorl" group the ridges make a circular pattern. The ridges in the "arch" group slope upward as they cross the fingertip. The fourth group is known as "accidental" because this pattern has no fixed form. Today, we use computers to classify and compare fingerprints.

Our Bodies

WHAT YOU NEED

paintbrush

markers

small plastic containers

colored paper

paints

Crazy fingerprints!

1 Mix paints in the containers to make different colors.

2 Paint your fingertips with the colors.

3 Press your fingertips onto the paper to make patterns.

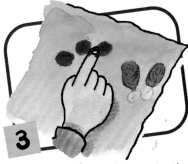

4 Create insects and animals by adding eyes and legs with the markers.

Make funny characters with your fingertips. Try handprints too!

Beautiful butterflies

Happy cats

Frantic frogs

7

Joints and levers

Watch a runner sprint along a racetrack and leap over a hurdle. Follow the moves of a dancer, curling and bending in an energetic performance. Watch an acrobat or gymnast make moves with their bodies that seem almost impossible: jumping, cartwheeling, or doing flips in the air. All of these athletes are using body movement.

Bending skeleton

The human body is made up of many different bones which are linked together in a framework, called a skeleton. The places where the bones fit together are called the joints. Most joints, such as those in our legs and arms, allow the bones to move.

Different kinds of joints

Some joints, such as our elbows, knees, and knuckles, work like a door hinge or lever. They are called hinge joints. Other joints, such as our wrists, ankles, and backbones, or vertebrae, are called ball and socket joints. In ball and socket joints, the end of one bone turns in the hole at the end of another bone. Ball and socket joints allow parts of our body to twist or swivel. The different types of joints let our skeleton bend and stretch in many ways.

Muscle pairs

The bones that meet at each joint are moved by muscles. Tendons connect muscles to bones. Muscles work in pairs. Muscles move bones by contracting, or shortening, themselves, and stretch out when another muscle pulls them back.

Our Bodies

Lively acrobats

Connect the joints to make a bending body mover

1 On a piece of poster board, draw outlines of different body parts. Look at the shapes shown at right to help you.

2 Decorate the body parts using different patterns and colors.

3 Carefully cut out the separate pieces.

4 Make holes in the body parts with a pencil point. Join the parts together with paper fasteners.

You can move your acrobat into all kinds of positions.

9

Eye-opener

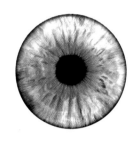

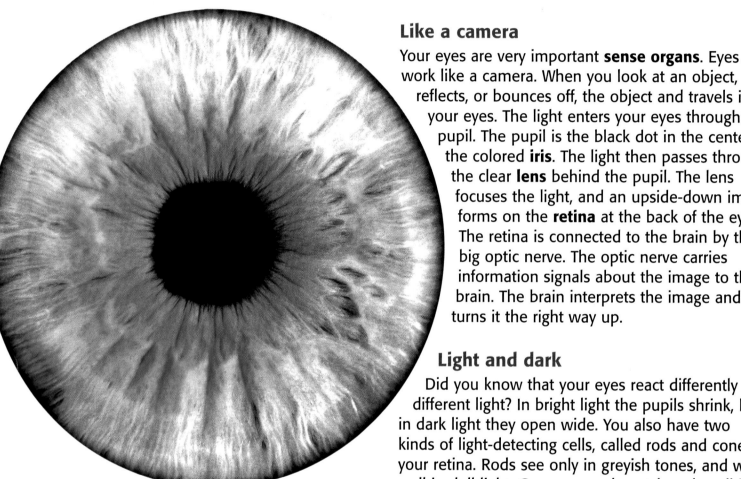

id you know that about 70 percent of the information you store in your brain is in picture form? Your eyes collect information about the world around you as thousands of different kinds of images. These images include the words you read, as well as the things you look at. Most of what you know comes from seeing.

Like a camera

Your eyes are very important **sense organs**. Eyes work like a camera. When you look at an object, light reflects, or bounces off, the object and travels into your eyes. The light enters your eyes through the pupil. The pupil is the black dot in the center of the colored **iris**. The light then passes through the clear **lens** behind the pupil. The lens focuses the light, and an upside-down image forms on the **retina** at the back of the eye. The retina is connected to the brain by the big optic nerve. The optic nerve carries information signals about the image to the brain. The brain interprets the image and turns it the right way up.

Light and dark

Did you know that your eyes react differently in different light? In bright light the pupils shrink, but in dark light they open wide. You also have two kinds of light-detecting cells, called rods and cones in your retina. Rods see only in greyish tones, and work well in dull light. Cones see color and work well in bright light. Each retina has about 120 million rods and about seven million cones.

Eye wash

Every time you blink, your eyelids wash tears across your eyes. Blinking cleans and protects your eyes. When you cry, some tears flow into the two tiny **tear ducts** in the corners of your eyes, then into the back of your nose. This is why you sometimes get a runny nose when you cry.

Our Bodies

WHAT YOU NEED

painted cardboard

scissors

pencil

glue

glitter

colored acetate

tissue paper

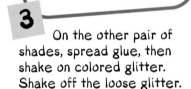

Make your own designer sunglasses

1 Draw two wacky-shaped frames on cardboard. Add arms, fold them back and cut out.

2 Bunch up bits of different colored tissue paper into little balls, and glue them onto one pair of shades.

3 On the other pair of shades, spread glue, then shake on colored glitter. Shake off the loose glitter.

4 Glue pieces of acetate onto the back of both pairs of shades for the lenses.

11

Black, white, and yellow

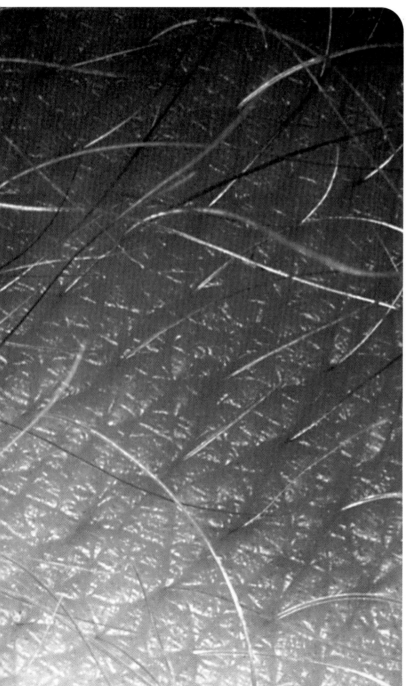

O ur skin is the largest body organ we have. Skin covers us completely and protects our inside parts. The color of our skin depends on how much melanin it contains. Melanin is a brown pigment, or coloring, which is formed by cells called melanocytes in the outer layer of our skin.

Melanin in the family

All people have about the same number of melanocytes in their skin. The melanocytes of dark-skinned people produce more melanin than those of light-skinned people. Your skin color is determined by your parents' skin color.

More melanin from sunlight

Melanin protects you against harmful rays from the sun. When you are outside, skin exposed to sunlight creates more melanin. This makes your skin a browner color. In some people, the melanin builds up to form spots, or freckles. More freckles appear on people's faces and hands because these are the parts which are exposed to the sun most often.

Protection

The best way to protect your skin from painful sunburns is to wear sunscreen when you go outside. It is also wise to stay indoors between 12 p.m. and 2 p.m., when the sun's rays are strongest.

A close-up photograph of skin.

Our Bodies

Multicultural collage

Create a fascinating collection of different-colored faces

1 Draw a shape on your poster board and cut it out.

Look in magazines and newspapers for pictures of people with different skin colors.

2

3 Cut out the faces, arrange them so they slightly overlap each other, and glue them to the poster board.

13

Keeping fit

JOHN WALMESLEY PHOTOGRAPY

In our modern, high-tech world it is easy to spend a lot of time in front of a TV or a computer. To stay healthy, your body needs exercise. Getting involved in sports is a fun way of keeping fit. It also allows you to be with friends and to play on a team.

Staying healthy

If you exercise regularly, you will feel happier, healthier, and you will keep your body in shape. You will also have more energy, so you can work and study to the very best of your ability.

Strong muscles

Exercise helps to build and tone your muscles, making them firm and strong. This does not mean that you have to have big muscles, just efficient ones. Exercise also stretches your joints, making them stronger and more flexible.

Good exercises

Walking, running, and jumping makes your heart stronger, improves your **circulation**, and helps you to breathe properly. You can rollerblade, skip, swim, play football, or ride your bike. Most of these sports help you develop balance, hand and eye control, and an ability to think and plan quickly.

14

Our Bodies

Fitness freaks

Make figures doing pushups, handstands, and exercises

1 Cover the work surface with newspaper.

4 Wrap the strips of fabric, one by one, around the figure so that the wire is totally covered.

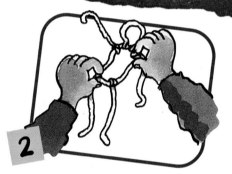

2 Cut long pieces of wire. Twist and bend them to form a rough but strong outline of an exercising figure.

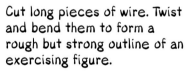

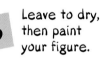

5 Leave to dry, then paint your figure.

3 Mix the filler paste in the bucket or bowl, following the instructions on the package. Stir in the strips of fabric.

You could make a group of colorful dancers

15

Coils and curls

Look closely at your arms. Can you see the tiny hairs growing out of the skin? Hair protects your skin and helps keep you warm. Hair grows all over your body, but most thickly on your head. You have about 100,000 hairs growing from your head!

Dead or alive?

Hair is made from **keratin**, the same material that helps make your nails. Hair grows from tiny holes, called hair follicles, in your scalp. Each hair is rooted inside its own follicle. Only the base of the hair, where it is growing, is alive. The strand above the skin surface is dead. This is why cutting your hair does not hurt.

Hair not only grows on your head, but it can also be cut to make wigs for other people. This girl from China is wearing a wig made from human hair for a festival.

Hair all over

There are small fine hairs all over your body. The only hairless parts of your body are the palms of your hands, the pads of your fingers, and the soles of your feet.

Style it right!

Your hair can be cut, shaped, decorated, twisted, and twirled! How a person's hair looks is an important part of their appearance. For hundreds of years, people have enjoyed creating all kinds of different hairstyles.

Inherited hair

The kind of hair you have depends on the shape of your hair follicles. Oval follicles make wavy hair. Round follicles produce straight hair, and flat follicles make curly hair. You usually inherit the kind of hair you have from your parents.

Our Bodies

clay

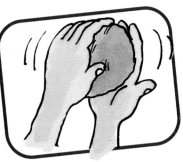

scissors

wool

silver paper

twigs

Plasticine

Hairy head models

Create your own salon of hairstyles!

1 Soften the clay by rolling it in your hands.

2 Make a head shape.

3 Cut equal pieces of wool and tie them together in the middle with another piece of wool to make a woolly wig.

4 Repeat step 3, using strips of silver paper.

Stick small twigs onto Plasticine to make a mohawk haircut!

Find different materials to make your hairy wigs

17

Sharp edges

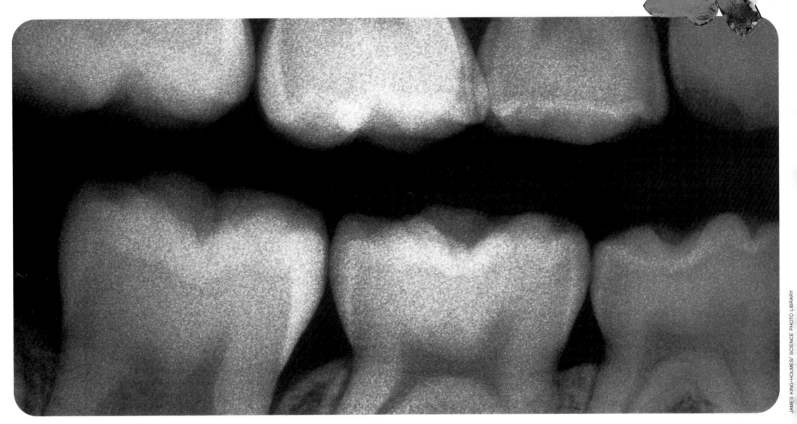

JAMES KING-HOLMES/ SCIENCE PHOTO LIBRARY

When you are born, your teeth are hidden inside your gums. Your teeth begin to push through your gums when you are about six months old. At about three years old, you have 20 baby teeth, which begin to fall out when you are five or six. By the time you are grown up, 32 strong adult teeth have replaced the baby teeth.

Strong stuff

Your teeth are covered by enamel, the hardest material in the body. Strong roots anchor your teeth into your jawbone, so they can withstand many years of grinding, chewing, and chomping!

Cut, crush, and chew

Look in your mouth to see your three different kinds of teeth. The sharp, flat incisors at the front cut and slice. The pointed canines next to the incisors grip and tear. The wide, flat molars at the back of your mouth crush and chew. Your teeth all work together to make sure your food is broken up into little pieces before you swallow.

Keep brushing

Brush your teeth after every time you eat! If you do, your teeth will stay healthy and strong. If you don't, tiny pieces of food stuck in your mouth will harm your teeth and gums. Remember to visit your dentist for regular checkups to keep your teeth healthy!

Our Bodies

WHAT YOU NEED

paints and brush

black marker

colored poster board

white cardboard

tissue paper

pencil

glitter

glue

scissors

1 Draw the outline of a monster face and hands on a piece of colored poster board.

2 Cut out the hands, face, and an opening for the mouth. Glue onto poster board.

3 Create sharp teeth by cutting triangular shapes from white cardboard. Glue the teeth into the monster's mouth.

4 Cut sharp claws and horns from the cardboard and glue these onto your picture.

5 Roll up a thick piece of tissue paper to make a padded nose.

6 Cut shapes from tissue paper and cardboard for the eyes and glue onto the face. Use a black marker to outline the eyes.

Make a family of toothy monsters

Use paints, glitter, sequins, foil, buttons, and bottle caps to create different monster faces.

Taste buds

Do you realize how amazing your tongue is? As well as helping you talk, your tongue guards your body from harm by letting you know whether the food or drink you are about to swallow is good or bad for you. If something tastes bad, your tongue warns you not to swallow it!

Working together

Together your nose and tongue detect, or sense, the different chemicals in food and drink. Tiny smell sensors in the back of your nose, and taste buds on the surface of your tongue, send messages along your nerves to the brain. Your brain interprets the messages and lets you know whether the flavors are delicious or disgusting.

Sweet or sour?

About 10,000 tiny taste buds are scattered across the surface of your tongue. Taste buds at the back of your tongue react to bitter flavors, and are the most sensitive. Taste buds on the sides of your tongue recognize sour and salty tastes, while the taste buds on the tip of your tongue pick up sweetness. The sensors in your nose also help you to determine how a food will taste. Try this: put on a blindfold, hold your nose, and taste something salty, something sweet, and something sour. Which flavor is which?

Mobile muscle

Your tongue is a muscle that wiggles, stretches, twists, and turns! The tongue helps to squash and move food around in your mouth. It removes food that gets stuck, and pushes chewed food to the back of your throat for swallowing. Your tongue also helps you shape the sounds of speech. Try this: hold the tip of your tongue and say something. Now what was that you said?

Taste buds magnified many times.

Our Bodies

Salt dough fruit basket

WHAT YOU NEED

3 cups (750 mL) flour

1 teaspoon (5 mL) oil

1 cup (250 mL) water

1 cup (250 mL) salt

paints and brush

baking tray

bowl and spoon

rolling pin

varnish

plastic bag

1 Put the oil, water, salt, and flour in a bowl and mix with a spoon to form the dough.

2 Knead the dough and place it in a plastic bag for one hour.

3 Roll out the dough. Make a basket shape and fill it with different fruit shapes. Place the dough shapes on the baking tray.

4 Bake in the oven for about one hour at 250 °F (150 °C). Ask an adult for help!

5 Leave to dry for a day and then paint. Add a coat of varnish to stop the baked dough from flaking.

Bake and decorate a selection of tasty glazed dough foods

21

Micro invaders

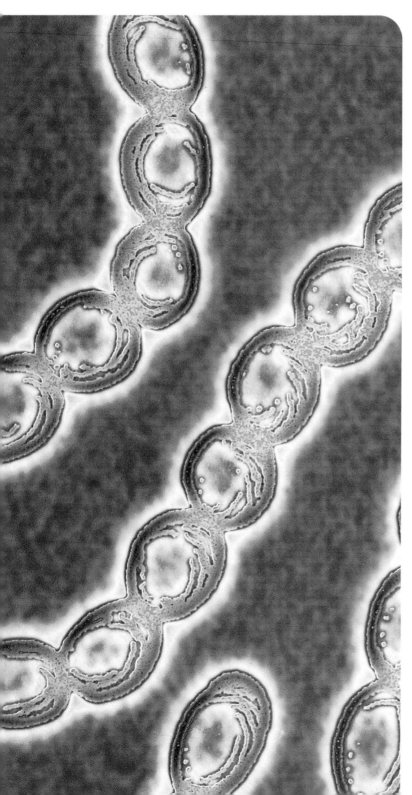

Germs shown through a microscope.

Germs are so small that you need a microscope to see them. Most of the time, you don't even know germs are around. Germs float in the air, on water, and are even found in food. When certain germs get inside your body, they can make you sick.

Good and bad

Bacteria are tiny, one-celled bodies, or organisms. Bacteria stay alive by feeding on their surroundings, and that could even be inside you! Bacteria can be good or bad for you. Some bacteria keep your digestive system healthy and fight off other germs. Other bacteria cause **infections** and illnesses.

It's catching!

A virus is a germ that travels from person to person in drops of water sprayed out of your mouth and nose when you cough or sneeze. If a virus gets into your **bloodstream**, it can quickly make you ill. Chickenpox and mumps are two fast-spreading illnesses caused by viruses. You usually only catch these viruses once. When you are ill, your body makes special defense cells, called **antibodies**. Antibodies attack the virus and will recognize and destroy it if it returns.

Fighting back

Antibiotic medicines fight illnesses caused by bacteria, and injections, or needles, called immunizations fight dangerous viruses. You can stop bad germs from getting inside your body by washing your hands often, especially before eating.

Our Bodies

paints and brush

scissors

craft wire

poster board

large sequins

gold thread

needle

Sequin chains

1 Make holes in the ends of each sequin with a needle.

2 Cut small pieces of wire. Link the sequins together by threading a piece of wire through the holes, making a loop in the center. Twist the edges of the wire around the center of the loop.

3 Cut a strip of poster board and paint it. Poke a row of holes along the bottom.

4 Thread the sequins onto the poster board.

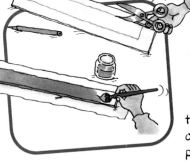

Try making a dangling chain curtain with beads and buttons

Poke two more holes in the top of the poster board and insert a piece of gold thread. Knot the ends. Hang the chain from a window and watch how the sun reflects patterns around the room.

23

Making faces

If you look at the faces of people in a crowd, it is easy to spot the differences between them. Different people have different facial features. Each person's eyes, nose, cheekbones, and mouth look slightly different. Facial features are **hereditary**, which means they can be traced back through the family.

Blue eyes, brown eyes

Why do some people have blue eyes and others brown? Eye color is determined by how much melanin the cells in your eyes produce. The more melanin, the darker your eye color. The amount of melanin your cells produce is passed on from your parents.

Smiles and frowns

Smiles and frowns, as well as all other movements of the face, are made possible by the facial muscles. There are more than 50 muscles in your face. These small muscles pull in many different directions.

Noses

Noses are big or small, wide or thin, hooked or straight. Your nose warms, cleans, and moistens the air you breathe before it reaches the lungs. Nerve endings at the back of your nose work as sensors to detect smells.

Our Bodies

Funny faces gallery

You can also create a funny faces gallery using family photographs

Make sure you ask permission before cutting up a photograph that does not belong to you.

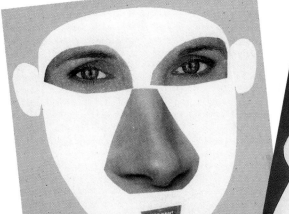

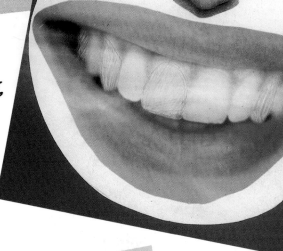

1 Cut out different eyes, noses, mouths, and ears from magazine pictures.

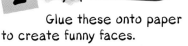

2 Glue these onto paper to create funny faces.

3 Draw an outline of a face around each funny face and cut them out.

4 Mount your gallery of faces on a piece of poster board.

25

Beating hearts

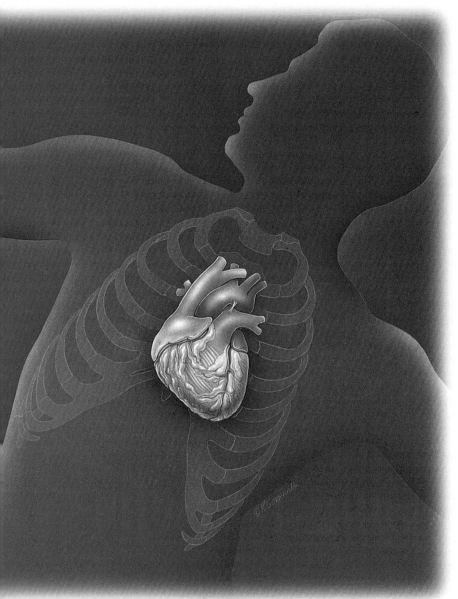

Super muscle

Your heart is a muscle about the size of your fist. Its job is to pump blood throughout your body. The heart works by squeezing and then relaxing, in rhythmic beats. Each beat of your heart pushes blood through a system of tubes made up of **veins** and **arteries**. Through these tubes, blood carries **oxygen** and **nutrients** to all the cells in your body.

Pumping blood

Your heart is made up of two pumps, side by side. The pump on the left side receives fresh, oxygen-rich blood from the lungs and pumps it around your body. This blood passes the oxygen throughout the body and carries away the **carbon dioxide** that your cells cannot use. The blood then returns to the pump on the right side of the heart where the used blood is sent to the lungs. In the lungs, waste carbon dioxide is removed and more oxygen is added. Now the blood is fresh again, ready to be pumped inside your body once more.

Heart beat

You can hear the beat of a baby's heart when it is still inside its mother's womb. The heart begins to beat about seven months before a baby is born. You can feel how fast your own heart is beating by pressing your fingers on the inside of your wrist. This is called taking your pulse. Your heart beats faster or slower depending on what you are doing. When you are asleep, your heart beats slowly. When you are running, your heart beats faster to increase the oxygen supply to your body.

Some muscles in your body work all by themselves without you realizing it. These muscles are called involuntary muscles. Your heart is an involuntary muscle that works all of your life, without stopping.

Felt cushion

Make a soft cushion decorated with hearts

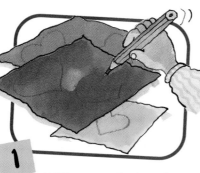

1 With a pencil, draw two large hearts on one color of felt, and two more hearts on a second color of felt. Draw one small heart on a third color of felt. Cut them out.

2 With colored thread, stitch the heart shapes onto a large square piece of felt.

3 Sew on sequins for decoration.

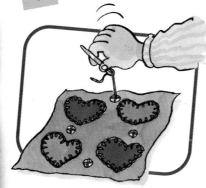

4 Stitch three sides of the felt square to another felt square that is the same size.

5 Stuff the inside of the cushion with cotton batting, then stitch together the last side.

27

Touch and feel

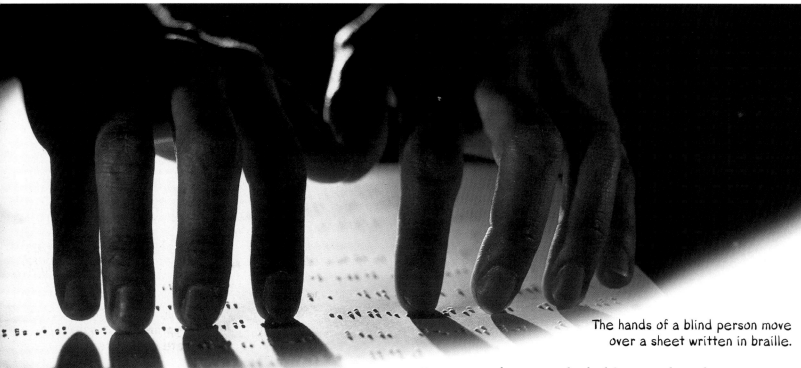

The hands of a blind person move over a sheet written in braille.

How do you know when something is too hot or too cold? By touching it of course! If you could not see or hear, your sense of touch would help you to understand the world around you. Try this: put on a blindfold and ask a friend to give you three different objects. Can you recognize the objects, just by touching them?

Layers of skin

Your sense of touch comes from the layer of skin called the dermis. The dermis is filled with tiny sense receivers, called receptors. Each receptor is connected by nerves to your brain.

Receptors detect, or feel, things such as heat, roughness, or pain, then send a message through the nerves to your brain.

Extra-sensitive

The receptors are spread unevenly through the dermis. You have more receptors in some areas of your skin than in others. For example, the skin on your lips detects heat more strongly than the skin on your elbows. Your fingertips are one of the most sensitive skin surfaces you have.

Touch and read

Blind people can read with their fingertips, using braille. Braille is a series of raised dots punched in paper. Blind people run their fingertips across the different patterns of dots. Each pattern stands for a different letter or number.

Our Bodies

Textured touch art

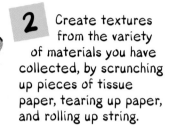

WHAT YOU NEED

- tissue paper
- sponge
- corrugated cardboard
- styrofoam
- tin foil
- glue
- cotton balls
- sand
- hay
- string
- pencil
- scissors
- poster board

1 Sketch a patterned outline on your poster board.

2 Create textures from the variety of materials you have collected, by scrunching up pieces of tissue paper, tearing up paper, and rolling up string.

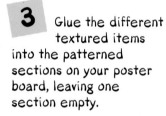

3 Glue the different textured items into the patterned sections on your poster board, leaving one section empty.

4 Put glue on the empty section and sprinkle sand onto it to create a rough texture.

How many different textured items can you find around your house?

Throwing and catching

Hand-eye coordination

When you throw or catch something, the brain acts as a coordinator between your eyes and your hands. Being able to catch or throw well depends upon this hand-eye coordination.

Brain work

In order for you to catch a ball, your brain has to work like a computer. When you see the ball coming, your eyes send messages to your brain. From these signals, the brain works out where the ball is and how fast it is moving. The brain uses this information to move your arms and hands into position, and then to control your fingers so they catch the ball.

Whenever we pick up a ball, it is hard to resist throwing it up and catching it. It seems such a natural thing to do! Many ball games, such as baseball, football, basketball, and rugby, involve throwing and catching. It looks easy enough, but it takes a lot of brain work to coordinate the eyes that see the ball with the hands that catch it.

Throwing

When you throw a ball, your eyes send signals to the brain, which works out how far away the catcher is, and then how much throwing power your arm must use. Your brain also calculates how fast you have to throw the ball, and in which direction the ball will travel. Signals are then sent to the arm and hand, so they move in the right way to hurl the ball through the air toward the catcher.

Our Bodies

Papier-mâché balls

Make and decorate a colorful collection of balls for catching and throwing games

WHAT YOU NEED

paints and brush

newspaper

bucket

paste and brush

1 Tear strips of newspaper and soak them overnight in a bucket of water.

2 Squeeze as much water as you can from the soaked paper.

Try juggling with small tennis ball-sized balls!

3 Dip the paper into the paste and shape it into a ball.

4 When it is dry, paint your ball.

Paint each ball a different eye-catching pattern or color.

31

Brainbox

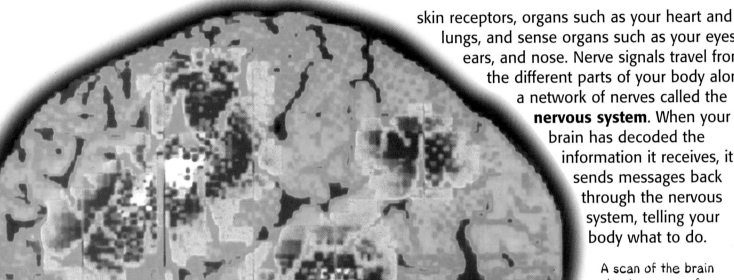

skin receptors, organs such as your heart and lungs, and sense organs such as your eyes, ears, and nose. Nerve signals travel from the different parts of your body along a network of nerves called the **nervous system**. When your brain has decoded the information it receives, it sends messages back through the nervous system, telling your body what to do.

A scan of the brain showing areas of activity during speech.

WELLCOME DEPT. OF COGNITIVE NEUROLOGY/ SCIENCE PHOTO LIBRARY

You are the owner of an amazing personal computer – your brain! Your brain controls every part of you by making a series of connections. It helps you smile, cry, think, and blink. Your brain solves problems, tells you how to move your arms and legs, and lets you know if you are hot or cold. It will help you remember the facts on this page!

Sending and receiving

Your brain never stops working. It receives information about the world around you, all the time. The information comes as **nerve signals** sent from your

Brain parts

Your brain looks something like a large, crinkly walnut! It is protected by your hard, bony skull. Your brain is divided into three main parts. Each part has a job to do. The largest and most important part is called the cerebrum, which controls ideas, feelings, and memories. The cerebellum is the smaller part that looks after balance and movement. The part called the brain stem connects the brain to the **spinal cord**. The brain stem holds the network of nerves that carries messages inside your body.

Left or right?

Are you right-handed or left-handed? Your cerebrum is divided into two sides – left and right. One side usually has more control than the other. For left-handed people this is the right side, while for right-handed people it is the left side.

Circuit board collage

pencil

poster board

gold and silver paints

paints and brush

tissue paper

glue

textured paper

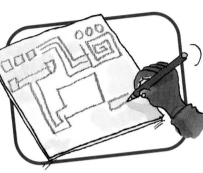

1 Draw a rough outline of your circuit board on a square piece of poster board.

2 Glue strips of different textured paper and twisted tissue paper around the outline to create circuit lines.

3 Paint bright colors along the lines. Use the gold and silver paint in the boxed areas of your circuit board.

Jazz up your circuit board with buttons, paper clips, and foil

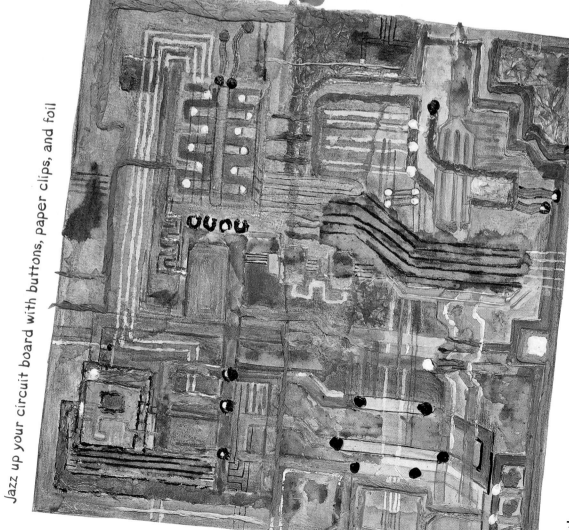

33

Pipes and tubes

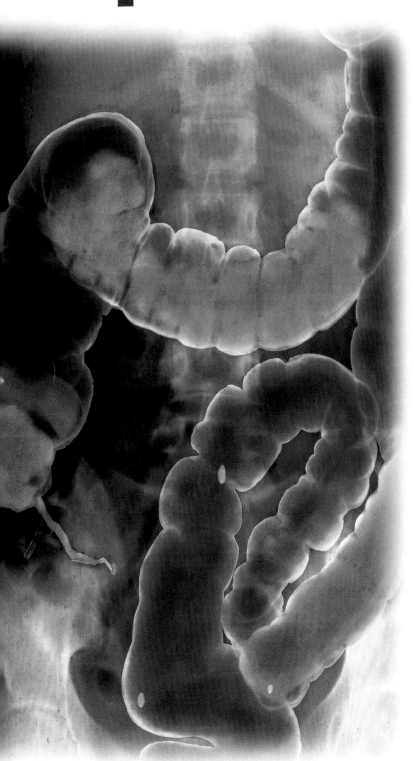

Did you know that after you have chewed and swallowed your food, it goes on a long journey to different parts of your body? On the way, food is **digested**, or broken down, into nutrients and energy for the body.

Softening saliva

Before you swallow, your food is mixed with watery saliva. Saliva flows out of tubes inside your mouth called salivary ducts. Saliva softens the food, and begins to break it down to make it easier to swallow and digest.

Squeeze and churn

After swallowing, the food moves down your throat into your **stomach**. Inside the stomach, food mixes with **gastric juices**, which contain chemicals called enzymes that break down the food even more, so it can be taken in by your body. Your stomach muscles squeeze and churn the food for up to six hours, until it is a soupy mixture. It is then squeezed through a long, winding tube called the small intestine, where tiny bits are taken into the blood and carried around your body.

Waste disposal

The parts of food that your body cannot use are then pushed through another long, coiled-up tube called the large intestine. Solid waste, called feces, is stored in a part of the large intestine, called the colon. Waste water, called urine, is sent from the **kidneys** to your **bladder**. When you go to the toilet, the waste squeezes out of your body.

An X-ray of the large intestine.

Our Bodies

Shimmering straw art

WHAT YOU NEED

straws

paints and brush

glue

construction paper

scissors

glitter

gold paint

sequins

pipe cleaners

1 Paint a background on construction paper using red, orange, and gold paints.

2 Cut the straws in different lengths and decorate them with glitter and twisted pipe cleaners.

Create pipe art with decorated straws

3 Glue the straws to the paper in a variety of patterns.

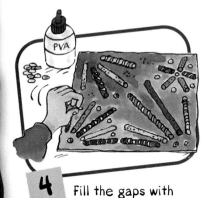

4 Fill the gaps with sparkling sequins.

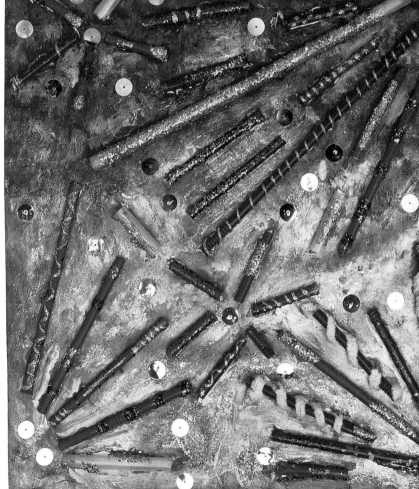

35

Breathing machine

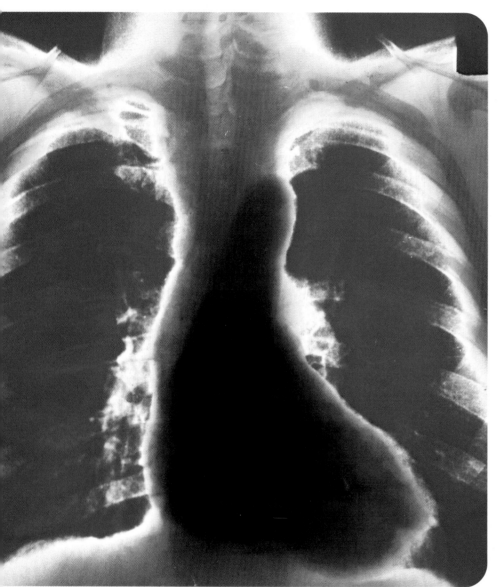

CNRI SCIENCE PHOTO LIBRARY

Working lungs

Your lungs are two large, sponge-like bags, or sacs. Each lung contains millions of tiny spaces, called air chambers. The spaces in your lungs fill with air when you breathe in, and empty when you breathe out. Lungs are protected by your bony **rib cage**, which moves in and out as your lungs take in oxygen and breathe out carbon dioxide. Each lung can hold as much air as a medium size balloon.

Important gas

Every part of your body needs oxygen. Your heart, blood, and lungs work together to make sure that oxygen is carried throughout your body. Your body cannot store oxygen, so it needs a constant supply. Each time you breathe in, air containing oxygen enters your nose, goes down your **windpipe**, and into your lungs. In your lungs, **blood vessels** absorb, or soak up, the oxygen. Your heart then pumps the oxygen-filled blood inside your body.

Making noises

How do you talk and make other sounds? Air from your lungs is pushed through the opening in your voice box, or larynx. The larynx looks like a box, with two pieces of skin stretched over it called the vocal cords. When air pushes on the lower vocal cords, they vibrate to make sounds. To feel the sounds your vocal cords make, place your fingers at the bottom of your neck and say "Ahhh!"

Every time you breathe you are taking in the oxygen your body needs to stay alive, and getting rid of the carbon dioxide it cannot use. You have two organs inside your chest specially designed for breathing. These organs are your lungs.

Our Bodies

Puffing bellows

1 From the cardboard, draw and cut out two bellow shapes as shown above.

2 Cut a strip of material to fit over the cardboard pieces.

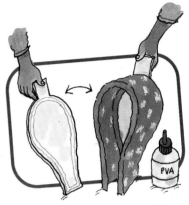

3 Glue the material at right angles to the two pieces of cardboard so that they are joined together by the material in the middle.

4 Draw and cut out the top for the bellow as shown. Fold along the lines.

5 Tape the top together, then glue it onto the bellows.

How much air can you make?

6 Paint and decorate the outside of your bellows with glitter.

Blood-red

id you know that you have about four quarts (4 L) of blood flowing around inside you? Blood speeds throughout your body via a system of tubes. The blood delivers nutrients, oxygen, and heat to keep your body alive.

Red and white blood cells, seen through a microscope.

Transportation system

Blood travels in your body in small tubes called blood vessels. Thick, muscular blood vessels, called arteries, carry blood that is filled with oxygen. Softer, stretchy blood vessels, called veins, carry the blood without oxygen. Your heart is the engine that powers the whole system. The right side of the heart pumps blood to your lungs to collect fresh oxygen. The left side of your heart pumps the oxygen-filled blood all throughout your body.

Blue blood

Look at the veins on the inside of your wrist. Why are they a bluish color? Veins look blue because your blood changes to a dark blue color as it releases oxygen into your body. When your blood collects oxygen from your lungs, it turns bright red.

What is blood?

Blood is a mixture of tiny cells floating in a fluid called plasma. One drop of blood has about 2,000,000 red blood cells, about 5,000 white blood cells, and about 2,500 cell parts called platelets. The tiny red blood cells carry the oxygen around your body. The bigger white blood cells attack harmful bacteria in your blood, and make antibodies to fight diseases. When you have a scrape on your knee, the platelets collect together to clot, or thicken, the blood to stop the bleeding.

Our Bodies

paints and brush

toothbrush

glitter

newspaper

colored paper

glue

poster board

Splatter painting

Experiment with string and straws to create more splatter art

1 Place newspaper down before you start. Put your paper on top of the newspaper.

2 Water your paint down, dab the paintbrush into it, and flick your wrist to splatter colors onto the paper.

3 Use a dry toothbrush to create a fine spray of paint.

4 Make circles on the paper with the glue and sprinkle glitter onto them.

5 Mount your splatter paintings on the poster board.

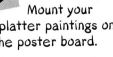

The inside picture

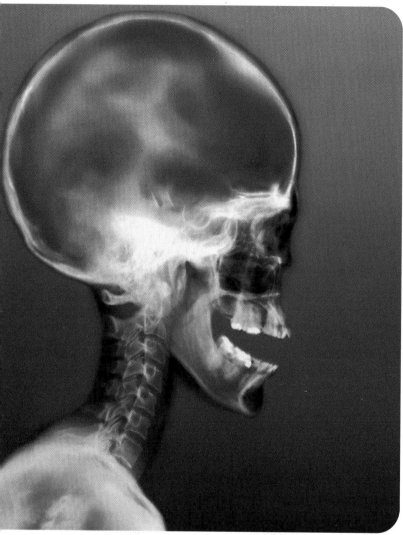

Invisible waves

An X-ray is a stream of waves of **electromagnetic radiation**. These invisible waves are like the light waves that come from the Sun, only shorter in length. Unlike sunlight, X-rays can travel through materials such as skin. This means we can use X-rays to see inside the human body.

X-ray photographs

Radiography is the use of X-rays to photograph the insides of things. Doctors use radiography to locate problems such as bone damage or tooth decay. Radiography can even be used to build a 3D image of the body that shows organs, blood vessels, and any diseased parts.

Checking up on bones

If doctors want to check how a child's bones are growing, they sometimes take X-rays of the child's wrists. If wrist bones look right on the X-ray, it is likely that all the other bones in the body are also growing correctly.

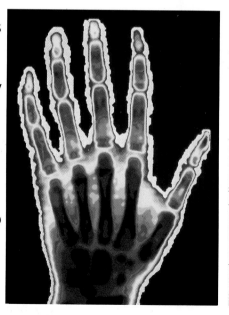

High tech uses

X-rays are also used to look for flaws in materials, to study crystals, and to find objects in outer space.

An X-ray shows all your bones.

If your skeleton suddenly disappeared, you would fall down in a heap! Your skeleton, which is made up of all the linked bones that lie under your skin, provides a strong frame for the whole body. The bones are joined together by joints, which allow the skeleton to move. Doctors photograph the skeleton using X-rays that let us see through the skin.

Our Bodies

X-ray art

You can create an extraordinary X-ray gallery of bony body pictures

white wax crayon

black paint or ink

paintbrush

tracing paper

1 Using a white wax crayon, draw the outline of a skeleton on tracing paper. Use the picture on the right as a guide.

Mix a little black paint and water together. Wash over the skeleton with watery paint to reveal your X-ray picture. **2**

3

Try creating skeleton pictures of different animals.

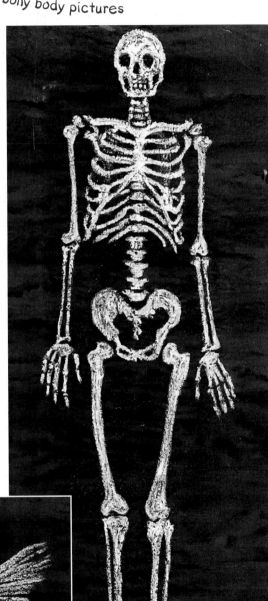

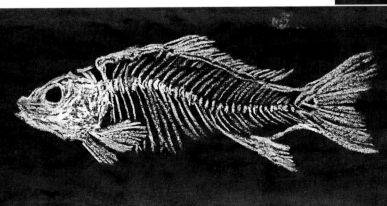

A see-through fish picture.

Sound catchers

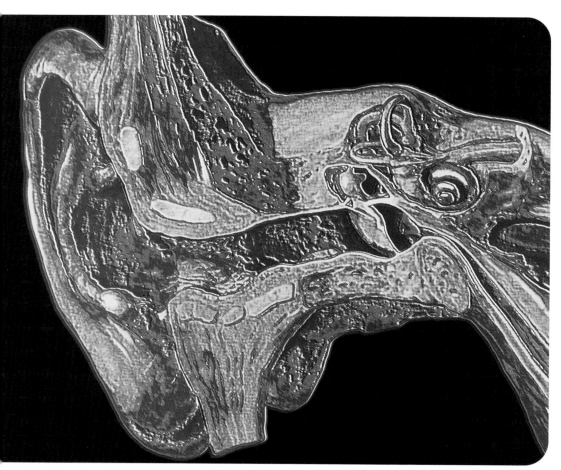

A computerized picture showing the structure of the ear.

Your ears collect information about the world around you. Not only can ears hear loud noises, such as crashing thunder, they can also hear soft sounds, such as a tinkling wind chime. Your ears are designed to catch sound as it moves through the air.

What's inside?

The human ear has three main parts. The ear flap is the part of your ear located at the side of your head.

The ear canal is the tube through which sound enters your ear. The ear flap and ear canal make up one of the main parts, called the outer ear. The outer ear is funnel-shaped, so **sound waves** can enter easily. The middle ear contains the **eardrum** and three tiny bones called **ossicles**. The inner ear, deep inside, contains the cochlea. Cochlea is a bony coil filled with fluid.

Sound waves

When sound waves enter your ear, they make the eardrum vibrate and the ossicles shake. The shaking ossicles cause the fluid inside the cochlea to move. These movements are detected by a nerve in the cochlea, which sends signals to tell the brain what you are hearing. Your ears react to different kinds of sounds. Listen closely to the noises around you. If a sound is very loud or irritating, how do your ears feel?

Balancing act

Your ears do more than help you hear. Ears also help you to balance. When you jump, skip, or run, the fluid inside your inner ear starts to swish around. As the fluid moves, it touches tiny nerve cells that send messages to your brain. Your brain then sends messages to your body to stop you from falling over!

Our Bodies

shells

wooden sticks

nail

thread or fishing line

Tinkling shell mobile

Add shining beads and buttons to make your mobile shimmer and jangle

1 Ask an adult to make a small hole in each shell with a nail.

2 Thread fishing line or thread through the holes in the shells. Knot each shell in place.

3 Place two wooden sticks together in a cross shape and tie with thread. Leave a long piece of thread so the mobile can hang from the ceiling.

4 Tie the strips of shells to the stick.

Hang your mobile near an open window, and listen to the sounds it makes as it tinkles in the breeze!

Body blueprint

In the days before computers, architects and engineers used hand-written plans or drawings of the work they had to do. These plans were known as **blueprints**. You also have a special set of instructions for each cell in your body. The human blueprint is found in the center, or nucleus, of the body's cells. Until recently only your fingerprints could identify you. Now we know that the structure of your special blueprint, or **DNA**, can also identify you.

Control centers

DNA stands for deoxyribonucleic acid, a substance containing the instruction code that determines how every person is built. The DNA molecule in each of our body's cells controls how the cell develops and operates. DNA provides a master plan for the whole body by passing information onto new cells.

DNA fingerprinting

The pattern, or sequence, of DNA in a sample of hair or body fluid, such as saliva or blood, can identify a person. DNA samples are sometimes used by police to help solve serious crimes.

Too small to see

A DNA molecule is so small that it can only be seen through a powerful microscope. DNA has a complicated structure that looks like two spirals joined together to form a twisted rope ladder. This shape is called the double helix.

This is a model showing the rope ladder structure of DNA .

WHAT YOU NEED

craft wire

gold thread

beads

sequins

Twisted choker

You can also make a twisted bracelet and a pair of earrings!

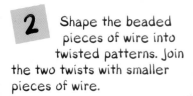

1

Thread the beads and sequins onto two pieces of craft wire. Tie a knot at the ends.

2 Shape the beaded pieces of wire into twisted patterns. Join the two twists with smaller pieces of wire.

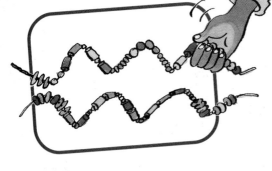

3

Attach small pieces of beaded wire across some of the sections, as shown. Twist the ends.

Tie gold thread onto each end of the beaded wire to finish your choker.

4

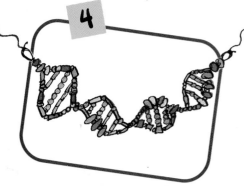

Glossary

antibodies Defense cells made in your blood that recognize and attack the germs that cause illness.

antibiotics Medicines made from molds or bacteria that help prevent disease.

arteries The blood vessels that carry oxygen-rich blood throughout your body.

bacteria Some kinds of bacteria live inside our body and help keep us healthy. Other kinds can cause disease and infection if they get inside us.

bladder The stretchy bag inside you, made of thin muscle, which fills up with urine. You empty your bladder when you go to the toilet.

bloodstream Blood as it circulates through the body.

blood vessels The thin, stretchy tubes that hold your blood. There are two main kinds: arteries and veins.

blueprint A plan that has every single piece of information needed to make something.

carbon dioxide One of the gases in the air we breathe, but which the body cannot use.

cells The living parts of you, which are so tiny you can only see them with a microscope.

circulation The movement of blood and gases around your body.

DNA The shortened name for deoxyribonucleic acid, the material found in the cells of everything alive. DNA determines exactly how we are built.

digestion Breaking down food into tiny nutrients.

eardrum The tight cover over the middle ear. It shakes when it is hit by sound waves.

electromagnetic radiation Waves of heat and light.

gastric juices The fluid made by your stomach that helps to break down food.

hereditary The word that describes a body feature you inherit, or get, from your parents or grandparents, such as blue eyes or curly hair.

immunizations Injections into the bloodstream that fight disease.

infection An illness caused by germs getting inside your body.

iris The colored part of your eyes.

keratin A tough substance made of protein that is found in the outer layer of your skin and which makes skin waterproof.

kidneys Two organs inside your body which are part of your digestive system. The kidneys separate the waste urine from useful liquid.

lens A soft, see-through part of the back of the eye which receives light.

ligaments Strong bands of tissue which hold the ends of bones and joints together.

marrow Soft material found inside the spongy layer of the bone that helps to make blood cells.

molecule The smallest piece of matter, consisting of one or more atoms.

nerve signals Messages that travel along the nerves of the body to the brain.

nervous system The system of nerves all over the body.

nutrients The part of food that helps us grow and stay healthy.

ossicles Three tiny bones – the stirrup, hammer, and anvil - in the middle part of the ear that vibrate with sound.

oxygen A colorless, odorless gas in the atmosphere which humans need to breathe.

retina The part of the eyeball that is connected to the brain.

rib cage The framework of ribs attached to the breastbone. The rib cage protects the lungs.

sense organs Parts of the body that help you see, hear, touch, taste, and smell.

sound waves When an object is struck, it vibrates, causing the surrounding air to move in waves that reach our ears.

spinal cord A thick group of nerve tissue that begins at the brain and continues down the backbone.

stomach The part of the body where food is broken down.

tear ducts The openings to the gland behind the eye which allow tears to flow to the eye.

tendons The tissue that connects muscle to bone.

veins The tubes in your body that carry blood back to the heart.

windpipe The pipe that lets air pass from the mouth and nose to the lungs.

Index

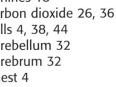

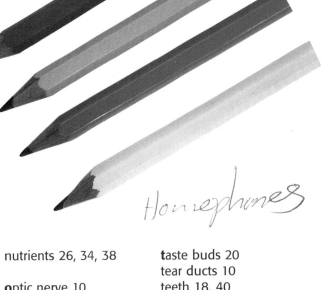

Homophones

Materials guide

A list of materials, how to use them, and suitable alternatives

gold foil

silver foil

filler paste

PVA glue

flour

salt

cellophane or acetate

The crafts in this book require the use of materials and products that are easily purchased in craft stores. If you cannot locate some materials, you can substitute other materials with those we have listed here, or use your imagination to make the craft with what you have on hand.

Gold foil: can be found in craft stores. It is very delicate and sometimes tears.

Silver foil: can be found in craft stores. It is very delicate, soft and sometimes tears. For some crafts, tin or aluminum foil can be substituted. Aluminum foil is a less delicate material and makes a harder finished craft.

PVA glue: commonly called polyvinyl acetate. It is a modeling glue that creates a type of varnish when mixed with water. It is also used as a strong glue. In some crafts, other strong glues can be substituted, and used as an adhesive, but not as a varnish.

Filler paste: sometimes called plaster of Paris. It is a paste that hardens when it dries. It can be purchased at craft and hardware stores.

Paste: a paste of 1/2 cup flour, one tablespoon of salt and one cup of warm water can be made to paste strips of newspaper as in a papier mâché craft. Alternatively, wallpaper paste can be purchased and mixed as per directions on the package.

Cellophane: a clear or colored plastic material. Acetate can also be used in crafts that call for this material. Acetate is a clear, or colored, thin plastic that can be found in craft stores.

 1 2 3 4 5 6 7 8 9 0   Printed in the USA   0 9 8 7 6 5 4 3 2